Messages to My Daughter

AF444217

Written by
Zahra Habib Hassan Al Darwish

Translation by
Fatma Yehia Hussein
&
Lola Abdulhag Salem

English LANGUAGE

Messages to my daughter

By: Zahra Habib Hassan Al Darwish

ISBN: 978-9948-04-964-7

First Edition – 2022

Published In United Arab Emirates

Permit No: MC-10-01-8594829

Age category: +13

PUBLISHERS

Books Frame FZE

Member of Emirates Publishers Association (EPA)

Publishing City Free Zone

Sharjah, UAE

Phone: +971 551361398

Email: info@booksframe.com

Bookstore: www.booksframe.com

Table of Contents

Zahra Habib Al Darwish Bio

Zahra Habib Al Darwish is an Emirati Women a multi-award-winning entrepreneur as the best event organizing company, best event planner, and business leadership excellence awards. She is a published Author and Novelist, a serial entrepreneur (founder of Sit Jump Play Event and BOXOUTUAE), an event planner, a motivational public speaker, an investor, and a passive income adviser/mentor.

Backed with study Zahra is holding a master of business administration and graduated with merit, as she studied smart cities and she chose Dubai as her dissertation topic., Hence, she did a computer science and computer engineering bachelor's degree. Also, Zahra worked for more than 13 years in the fields of banking, airlines, facility management, and insurance.

Being a mother of 4 made has changed her priorities for her child's best future, therefore, she wrote a book about the relationship between a mother and the first daughter. She is planning as well to be The Arab Agatha Agasty by writing a series of crime/ mystery novels.

Socially, she supports and empowers women, children's health, and cultural awareness in simple she empowers happiness. As per Zahra, she said: "empowerment never comes from outside it is always inside, but you have to know how to accelerate it and make it your power to catch the opportunities in your life."

Love you

Zahra Habib Al Darwish

Multi Award- Winner
Published Author and Novelist
A motivational Public Speaker
Investor – Passive Income Mentor
Founder and CEO Sit Jump Play Event
and BOXOUTUAE
Zahra.h.darwish@gmail.com /
0507989398

Social Media

WhatsApp: 0507989398
Website: http://www.sitjumpplay.ae

LinkedIn: https://www.linkedin.com/in/zahra-al-darwish-943295a6

Instagram:
https://www.instagram.com/zahra_al_darwish
(Personal)

Instagram:
https://www.instagram.com/sitjumpplayevent
(Business)

The Introduction

In this simple book, I want to express my feelings as a mother to my child, and for children from newborns to twelve years old.

I hope this book will be a guide and an evidence for mothers who the trick narrows them down, or who have gone through hard and difficult moments, and do not know what to do.

This book is a bridge between the mother and the daughter, especially the daughter who is attached to her mother; in order to identify her feelings and her mother's feelings at the same time, and maybe both of them will write down their words like a bell rings in a time of the obliviousness.

We live once, but we go through many experiences that may lift us to the top, or bring us down to the bottom. You are as a mother you must be there, and support them; to reach their destination.

I write my experience with my twelve-year-old daughter, and write down everything I have been through during all these years.

Advices, which must mothers, give them to her daughter at every stage.

Let's start . . .

"The glorious day has come, and we've begun to prepare to welcome you to this life, the moment which I see you in it in front of me and touch you, and feel your warmth".

The First Sight

How wonderful at first sight! Irresistible feeling, especially if the child is a firstborn. I am a mother for the first time, turned me from a woman to a mother, changed my life and my priorities, and made me see the life from a different perspective.

I became care about you, and I fear for you, this is the mother's instinct that Allah has bestowed upon us; to have mercy, love, and sacrifice for our livers and loved ones.

I got pregnant with you, and because of not following a healthy diet, I developed gestational diabetes, and suffered from it for five months of pregnancy, and due to health complications, the supervising doctor decided that I should do a caesarean section, not a natural birth.

The important thing is that I reluctantly agreed, especially that they measured your size inside my stomach, and you were much bigger than the normal size. It was a danger to your life and mine, so I did not want to take risks, and this is the reason that forced me to agree to a caesarean section, which is that you come out safely and without any health or physical complications...

The glorious day has come, and we've begun to prepare to welcome you to this life, the moment which I see you in it in front of me and touch you, and feel your warmth.

I entered the operating room, all my family were around me, and the operation succeeded, and I went out of the operation room to the post-operative room for observation.

After hours, I opened my eyes, and I saw blackness everywhere, and the ceiling of the hospital was very high, and everything was scary.

I remember starting to scream: Am I going to die? Or am I really dead? What is this? Where am I? I tried to get up, but I could not because of my abdominal pains after the operation, the pain was very frightening.

Suddenly I saw a light interspersed with a voice, the nurse's voice was telling me to calm down, and that I was frightening the people around me, and then I was sure that I was alive, and what I could feel was that I was not under anesthesia.

I slept tired and stressed, and woke up again. Where is my daughter? I want to see her. The nurse was very cruel, she said: stop bothering, I said: I have not seen my daughter yet, I want to see her! Where is she? Where? Then the nurse went with all his might, fetched my daughter, and left her away from me, not knowing that I could not get up because of the practical pains.

And she said: Here she is, take her, and stop screaming, and surely, she must say: (As if she is the only woman to give birth)!

I did not care for her, but I wanted to see you, I tried to sit despite the pain, and from afar, I saw you until you stopped screaming when you saw me, your eyes, your color and your shape.

You were like an angel, I could not help myself, I burst into tears, you are my daughter until I did not know what your name was, only my daughter. At that moment, no one knows this, but I promised to give you a good life, and what you want, I will make you study, educate, and provide you with a happy life.

I was talking to you from afar, so I could not carry you either until the evil nurse came back, took you from me and went, and said: she must go to the nursery, and I took you from me and went, and this was the first look, oh my darling.

"How wonderful is this feeling of fullness
and gratitude for all the blessings of Allah,
and of health and wellness".

Who is she?

After suffering at first sight, I saw you different and wonderful, you were crying, and you stopped crying and making noise when you saw me, then they took you from me with all cruelty.

This nurse I will never forget for the rest of my life because of her cruelty and lack of cooperation with me, and I was in the most difficult moments of my life.

From my tiredness and intense crying for the situation in which I am in, I fell into a deep sleep, and did not wake up until I heard my mother's voice. Then I saw my mother, my sisters and my husband, but my eyes were searching for one person among all these. I was looking for you, oh my darling, but I did not see you anywhere, and I asked them: Where is my daughter? They said to me: Yes, we will ask them to bring it to you, oh mother of Fatima (Umm Fatima)!

Umm Fatima? Who is Fatima? Her name is Fatima. What a wonderful and beautiful name after the name of the daughter of the Prophet - May God bless him and grant him peace -.

I was very pleased with the name, and I wished God to bless you with this name, and to gain the good qualities associated with this name.

I told my mother that I want to see my daughter, I did not see her well today, she is one day old, or she has not finished the day either, I want to see her. My brothers went, and told the nurse, they brought you to me, and I looked at you again, but this she is not who I saw yesterday.

But where is she? My family told me it was her! Who have you seen before? Everyone asserts that it is her: Perhaps you were delirious because of sedatives and anesthesia, I said: Perhaps. The important thing is that they gave me you, and with my hand I carried you for the first time in my life, and I am in full mental strength, I hugged you, I loved you, and I smelled you for the first time, how wonderful and different it was.

The feeling was great, but I still doubted: Why is she different?

Yesterday she was full, and her eyes were as if they were Chinese, because of her large cheeks, I could not see her eyes, nor could I preserve her features; because she was very fat, and because what I see now is weak and light as a breeze, and her cheeks are full but with limits. I could see her eyes, and contemplate them, I had to ask: Who is she?

The supervising doctor came, and I could not resist and I asked her, for sure I seemed to make her laugh a lot, and she said to me: She is your daughter, she is very beautiful, and she told me the reasons.

I asked the doctor who told me: Yesterday was the first day of her life, and due to complications of gestational diabetes, she was very swollen, and her weight was very high. But with the passage of time, and her exposure to the natural atmosphere, the swelling disappeared, and she returned to her normal weight, and she is now fine, and everything in her is normal.

How wonderful is this feeling of fullness and gratitude for all the blessings of Allah, and of health and wellness. I praised God on that day; because she did not take anything from me that did not suit her in terms of characteristics or diseases, thank God.

"Choose the nicknames well if you want, or be satisfied with the names; because the mother and father did not choose this name in vain, because the surname may be associated with your children for a lifetime".

Chucky

This is your first day complete; you are nicknamed Chucky, right? Aren't you curious, why were you given that name? Why Chucky? And what is Chucky at all?

There is little information about the scary game, which is a disheveled orange-haired boy who looks like a wizard, a series of scary movies in the 1990s, from the good old days.

Welcome all. The story is that a little boy gets a gift from his mother, a big and adorable doll, for his birthday. Since he got the doll, strange and frightening events have occurred in their house, which have no explanation.

With the days, the boy discovers that the doll Chucky is enchanted, and is inhabited by an evil wizard, and transformed into a soul inside the doll; Escape the police!

The boy discovered this, especially since the evil spirit wants to take him to a place, and turn his soul into a body; Because he needs it, otherwise his spirit will weaken, and die if the puppet continues to stay.

Why don't you watch the three-part movie, I think? Now that we know who Chucky is, and what he looks like, let's come to you, Fattum. Why are you called Chucky? All this from your aunt Laila, as soon as she saw you for the first time, she said: Oh my God, your daughter looks like Chucky! What? She said: Look, she is pure white, with rosy cheeks and full, and her hair is full and standing like thorns, and every time we try to get her hair down, it refuses to fall down, and he stands again, until she tried to wet it with water in a desperate attempt; to make it drop.

I said to your aunt: Where is the resemblance? She told me that Chucky is (cute), and that I love him; so, I will call it his name. I did not object, it's okay, and I said: This title will not last, but your aunt still calls you Chucky, and you love this title that stuck to you.

The days passed, and you grew up, and the nickname became more mentioned than your real name.

Your name is wonderful and dignified, it seems that it annoyed your father a lot, and I told everyone to stop calling you by that name, or at least not to call it so much that it overshadows your real name. Just stay between us. This is what happened, and out of love or pampering, some of your aunts call you Chucky.

From my point of view, I think that it is okay to nickname the ones we love, but nicknames should be comfortable to hear, and gain the approval of everyone, and that the nickname is not offensive, and we are ashamed of it, or we do not like it in the future, or it is something that causes embarrassment among people.

Choose the nicknames well if you want, or be satisfied with the names; because the mother and father did not choose this name in vain, because the surname may be associated with your children for a lifetime.

"Children are our livers, we tire of them, and they are in our bodies, and we tire of them by raising them and caring for them, and they are a trust for us from God; In order to improve their upbringing and education, and make them strong-willed and physically strong. The important thing is that we make them love God - Glory be to Him -; because he created them and honored them".

The love of Possessive

The love of possession is not limited to a lover and his girlfriend only, the love of possession is that my child is mine, only mine. I was so jealous of everyone who approached her, and everyone who talked to her, that I thought to myself: Oh my God! I need a doctor; I am not like this with my husband, nor with my mother or my family, so why has she become my whole life? And all I have?

When I heard people calling me (Umm So-and-so), I was overjoyed and proud of this name.

After her birth, I still suffer from postpartum complications, and I developed a sensitivity in my skin that always makes me under the sedative, and because of it I could not breastfeed her, as she is the only one without my three children. I did not breastfeed her. I feel guilty and oppressed, but this is the truth, I could not breastfeed her because of my health conditions...

Being under the sedative periodically after my birth, my husband tried to take care of my daughter by changing her clothes, such as pampers, milk and others. My daughter no longer needs me, her father is doing the homework, I found her around, and where have I been?

I could not stand what was happening, I could not, I just became hostile to everyone, because she is my daughter, and she is mine and no one else! My jealousy was the cause of many problems I had with my husband and family. I was staring, forgetting my pain and tiredness, until the day came and you were crying a lot, and you wanted to drink milk, and I was sleeping after I took my sleeping medicine, I heard your voice, and I got up, and made the milk for you.

Everything was normal, but thanks to God - Glory be to Him - your father came at the right moment, grabbed my hand, and prevented me from giving you milk, and I got angry a lot. Why? What do you mean by this work? Until he said: Give me your hand, and he poured a little milk on my hand, and it was boiling from the intensity of the heat, then I could not say anything, and my husband reprimanded me from doing it again, and took care of my health until I recovered, and then I would be able to take care of the baby and the house as well.

That night, though I was under the sedative, I could not sleep; I sat thinking to myself what if your dad did not come in time? What if I give you milk?

Oh My God! I was going to ruin your life, I would make you without a sound, and just thinking about all this made me cry in an unreasonable hysterical state.

I started praying to God to release me, and to protect you from all harm, and from that day I stopped being jealous, I stopped loving possession, and made the matter end smoothly and simply.

Here when you think about yourself and selfish, and jealousy flares up in you, you will find that you are alone, helpless, leave the matter smoothly, people with you are mocked by God for you; To help you, use the issue to your advantage, and deal with all transparency, they are there to help!

Children are our livers, we tire of them, and they are in our bodies, and we tire of them by raising them and caring for them, and they are a trust for us from God; In order to improve their upbringing and education, and make them strong-willed and physically strong. The important thing is that we make them love God - Glory be to Him -; because he created them and honored them.

I was afraid of the situation that made me stay away from her for a while until I reconciled with myself, and then everything went wonderfully calm.

I must mention that depression after childbirth and pregnancy is a reality, and its degrees and effects on the psyche vary, except, and we treat it either with drugs or with prayer, but, thank God, I quickly recovered from it.

"Self-actualization is a wonderful thing, but
priorities must be set and understood.
What does it mean to succeed in my work,
fail in my motherhood, and build an
independent, playful, and productive
family?"

The Beautiful Sleeper

How wonderful it is to realize yourself, to feel this self, and the success that will be achieved for you. This is what happened, I gave birth to you several months ago, the period of delivery has ended, and the time has come for seriousness and time for work, especially since I was employed in another job and with greater responsibility, I was the boss, ha-ha-ha. I had employees who took care of their affairs, and I was part of the management team, and my responsibility was to succeed, especially in a new emerging company, so the pressure was severe and visible to everyone.

You were in the third month, I was trying to remember it, but it was difficult for me because I was exhausted at work, you were like a beautiful sleeper. Early in the morning, I took you to your grandmother with all your kit, and I used to ask about you every moment, whenever I found an opportunity I called you, and asked about you. Sometimes I make my mom put you on the phone; to hear your voice, you were something confusing to me at the time.

How can I not live your moments, and rejoice with you? The important thing is that self-realization took all of my mind, and I didn't care about anything but success.

After a long day, I came to pick you up from your grandmother's house while you were sleeping. I change your clothes and diaper, kiss you until you are full, and hug you, and we sleep together until the morning, and you do not help that, and you are absent from sleep. I know you did not feel me, you do not feel my longing for you after a long day, and I did not want to wake you up; So that you do not get upset and disturb your sleep. The situation continued until you reached your eighth or ninth month, and every day you go to sleep, and come back to sleep, and we had no intimate moment between us at this time, the moment we gathered together, until the day came that shocked me at your grandmother's house, come, my darling?

You walked away from me like I was a monster, don't you want to?! Come to Mama! And you didn't want to.

In the end the maid tells you to come to me, and that I am your mother. The shock blew my mind.

From that day I decided to be only yours, I gave up everything, and decided to be with you; In order for you to be mine, raise you, and prepare you to serve your country, and I was hoping that God would enable me to do that.

My darling beautiful sleeper, Self-actualization is a wonderful thing, but priorities must be set and understood. What does it mean to succeed in my work, fail in my motherhood, and build an independent, playful, and productive family? Life is beautiful for those who understand it, as they say, and life is a musical and melodies, if the opportunity came, at least I was on the right path.

"My child and my work are the
most important thing in my life".

The Conflicting Feelings

The conflicting feelings are very strange, make your mind think of a thousand thoughts and ideas without realizing whether you are doing the right thing or not.

My troublemaker is a few months old, and her features began to stand out, and her beauty dazzled everyone who passed by, or caught her. Pure-hearted, dazzling, a wonderful sight that fascinates the heart.

At that time, I remember that I was at the head of my work, and I was responsible for employees, and I had to be an advocate for them and their rights at work.

My child, my work and my success are the most important thing in my life. I had to choose the most important on my priority list. At first, I could not differentiate because I was motivated for success and self-realization, but one day, a very simple situation that I went through with my child changed all my priorities...

I was at my mother's house visiting her with my child and the nanny, and when we finished eating, I wanted to pet my daughter a little, but she refused to come to me, she refused to look at me as if I was the stranger, and the maid found her who knew her, and I was nothing ... I was very surprised, and I felt uncomfortable.

What made the matter strange and narrow is that the nanny tells my daughter and says to her: Do not be afraid, go to her, she is your mother. At that time, I felt that there was no point in me if my daughter did not know me, and that others had to tell her and calm her down and let her know that she was my daughter.

I asked: What do I do?

Humiliation, work, and self-formation are important in life, but if this affects your priorities, you have to choose, and you can go back again when time is ripe for it.

I chose my daughter, to be her mother, to love me, and to know me as her mother. That is why I preferred to give up work, do what is required of me, raise my daughter, make her a child raised on a sound basis, and make her superior, happy, and balanced; To be an active member of society instead of being lost, not knowing who she is, and what her original nationality is.

"A person remains vigil and tries to find solutions to all the problems he faces".

E-commerce establishment

Sit Jump Play

After deciding to stay at home, and take care of you, my love, I decided to slow down a little, look; you were the reason for establishing my new e-commerce company (Sit Jump Play). When I was planning to resign, I thought about starting my own company; not to stop working completely. The search phase for a company to develop the electronic market for children's products has begun.

Do you believe this, my love? I made everything around me related to you; because you are my obsession and longing.

Indeed, I started contracting with all companies that produce children's products and essentials, and this matter opened up other challenges for me for self-realization. You were an integral part of my project, which I talk aboutin press interviews, radio, newspapers and magazines at the time.

I remember you as the one who showed me my way, you attended all my meetings and all my opponents, you were the basis. From that day on, I say: I must establish a company that will become yours, you and your brothers after me, and I will present it to you as a gift. A person remains vigil and tries to find solutions to all the problems he faces.

"It is really nice to take the advice of others, but not to trust it and rely on it for everything"

This is my brother

After you were born, it did not take long for me to get pregnant with your brother. You were always surprised by the size of my stomach when it grew up, and I was afraid to tell you that you would not be alone, but that there would be a brother who shares everything with you; so, I was waiting for the right time to tell you about it. Surely, I asked everyone who knew what would be the correct way to tell her?!

Some of them said make a party (baby shower) and tell her! And some of them said buy her a doll in the form of a boy, and let her play with him, spend time with him, and when you give birth, it will be normal for her!

As if I do not know you, ha-ha from your childhood to this day you do not like dolls, and when I bought you one you were on purpose to break it. For my part, I wanted to surprise her as if it was a gift to play with him, and not to be alone. Of course, I would from time to time and gradually read to her stories interspersed with a brother, cartoons interspersed with these stories.

Until the day I gave birth to your brother, and your brother Muhammad, who was very warm since his childhood, and brings reassurance and joy to everyone who looks at him. The first look for you was not with me because as usual, I am tired, and under anesthesia for a while. Your first look was with your father and family.

I did not know that you kissed your brother on the cheek, and you were looking at him with great astonishment, who is he? What is this rather? Until I woke up, and said to you, Come, and I sat you on the bed, and put your brother on your lap, and I introduced you to him: This is Muhammad, this is your little brother, and you are his older sister. Your responsibility now is to love and manipulate him, and to contain him. And I saw in your eyes that sparkle that bodes happiness, then I knew that your brother would be safe hahahaha.

We came home, and you were playing with him by putting your hand in his mouth, laughing, and having fun with him, sure by my supervision. Everything was wonderful; Because you are still in the circle of attention, but I felt that you started to get jealous when I sleep near him, and take care of him, especially when I was breastfeeding him, because I did not breastfeed you because of my health condition at the time.

I am still sorry my dear, forgive me. You were wondering about the subject, and I wanted you to ask me, what are you doing? But then you were in the sixth or ninth month of your life, unable to speak, but your eyes explain everything.

It seems that you did not accept the matter, and problems arose when your brother began to take your things, and you did not accept that this was yours, and we began to quarrel back and forth over the most trivial reasons. But after I asked my mother and everyone, I learned that it is a normal thing, not all children are comfortable with brothers, and some of them quarrel for trivial reasons.

Let us hope that when they grow up, they mature to be loving brothers, thank God.

It is really nice to take the advice of others, but not to trust it and rely on it for everything because in the end you have to appreciate what suits you, and work on that basis.

People's opinions may suit them, but not necessarily yours. Children are genders, they can accept or reject that, and most important of all, trust that God loves His servants, and the ties of kinship with them.

"This is how she became many friends, and he became a prince from the beautiful past that she remembers!"

Childhood Friends

I always thought she did not remember her childhood at all; because she is less talkative, and I thought I was trying to remind her of the past, but she remembers everything.

I asked: What do you remember? She said: Everything! Like what? I remember my friend Amir, and I remember we used to dress up as Spider man and I was the bat women, and we had a lot of fun in the cockroach house, lol. Yes, the cockroach house, it is another story I will tell you later. I remembered with her that they used to get up early, and she used to have breakfast in Amir's house, or in the inner corridor leading to our apartment, or at the Security man desk until lunchtime. They eat lunch, then take a nap in the afternoon, and then go to play again.

I can say: Their presence as our neighbors was an irreplaceable blessing, although I did not visit them, because the woman did not speak Arabic or English, but she cared for my daughter as if she were her own, and did not accept any harm to her. I was happy with them until the day they decided to leave to live in another place. I felt sad and upset, because their son was my daughter's first friend, and they were much attached to each other as if they were brothers, and it was very difficult for me to see her alone.

The day came, they took him, and I found my daughter sad, melancholy, and alone, looking for him, and knocking on their door, and asking for him.

I spoke to her to make her understand that life is like this, full of stories of parting and departure; we may or may not find them again. Do not grieve over what fate does, and what is written for you, my dear.

Not much passed until schools started, and I joined her in her current school at her young age, she was three years old, but I was sure that she was able to adapt to life.

This is how she became many friends, and he became a prince from the beautiful past that she remembers.

"They don't know the truth, but they trust us, and we don't lie, so let the choice be yours".

This Is My Clothes

I was selective, you like to search, and choose the clothes you like, and you do not like to interfere, or take something for you according to my taste. I was sometimes surprised that you are two years old, you have a strong personality, and you like to choose what you want yourself.

I loved it, the important thing is one day I was with you - my brat - shopping, buying new clothes, we were in the (Mall of the Emirates) a children's clothing store, and I think they closed the store now, it does not exist!

It was the beginning of summer, and your eyes fell on a white shirt and a fuchsia octopus, you liked it, for at that time I was studying you at home about animals and mollusks, including the octopus.

You insisted on the shirt, and I said: it's okay, so you chose pants that fit, a hat, shoes and a bag, and here we are.

We still need swimwear too, with slippers, shoes and Accessories for hair. You were very happy, my love, I have everything, I have an octopus hahahaha, and clothes and accessories are in your closet, and whenever we go to visit the mall or parties, you wear these clothes. At first I said: It's okay, the clothes are nice, and they look great on her, but that the topic is repeated every day and every moment, to wear the same clothes is a lot, a lot, my daughter...

Until I remember, your aunt once said to me: Do you have nothing but these clothes? I told her: Clothes fill the cupboard, but she only wants these clothes. It lasted - I think - for three months, we washed and dressed it until it changed its color.

O God...

I had to stop these behaviors someday. One day I took the clothes with all their accessories, put them in a plastic bag, and threw them behind the big cupboard so that no one could take them out at all. In the morning, I see you excited running to the wardrobe, looking for clothes, but you cannot find them. You went to the ironing room, and you did not find anything, as if the ground opened up and swallowed all your clothes, and you started - my love - crying and wailing.

I tried to understand that he disappeared, the octopus went to the sea, and he went with his friends and took clothes with him, and you were looking at me with teary eyes, and saying to me: Really, Mama? And I, oh, at that time my heart hurt so much, I should have lied to you, so I said: Yes - my love - he really went into the depths of the sea as I told you with his companions and family, and then she fell silent, did not cry, and said: It's okay, let him go, I have a lot of clothes...

I said: Thank you, God. What is the name of what I did? Is this the white lie that covers our mistakes? They do not know the truth, but they trust us, and we do not lie, so let the choice be yours. I leave the choice to you mom's. What do you think, should we do what I did or ignore the issue and continue with the child's stubbornness?

"We started unpacking the water fridge, and here was the surprise! Cockroaches made their home in the refrigerator, and when we opened it, the kitchen was full of cockroaches".

The Cockroach House

Yes, it is a strange name for a house that I can call the first marital home for me and my husband. It was a house, or rather an apartment consisting of a room and a hall. We were one of the first residents in the building. I got pregnant, gave birth to my daughter and son, and years later, every time we made juice, or drank water; we found a small cockroach in the cup.

My husband was looking around, and he did not find any cockroaches at all, the kitchen was very clean and fed up with its cleanliness; He was very surprised by the matter, so we said it was possible that the cockroach rose from the water mouth and fell, so we dismissed it.

A day came when I prepared milk for my three-year-old daughter, and she drank it, and she was enjoying it until I saw something black under the milk, so I took it from her and emptied the milk, and the shock was that it was a small cockroach! We kept looking, and searching, and sure I brushed her teeth, and got rid of the nurse, and I felt that what had happened was negligence on the part of the nanny, and I reprimanded her for that. The same thing happened to my baby son! Cannot, what is this? The kitchen is very clean; it smells of Dettol and hygiene, what is the matter? I began to think it was magic, and that someone had charmed my children. Make sense! Until the day, I asked my husband to change the water fridge to a new one, because the fridge suddenly stopped producing hot water, and I need it so much.

We started unpacking the water fridge, and here was the surprise! Cockroaches made their home in the refrigerator, and when we opened it, the kitchen was full of cockroaches, And I started screaming with the children, and I left the house to clean with the insecticide company, and I went to my mother's house for five days to solve the problem, and from that day we all remember that house, the cockroach house, and this is our memory of the four of us. My other daughters don't know, and don't understand, if we mention our old home.

"I Thank you —oh Allah- for your blessings and for your endless giving towards every mother, father and child".

School Interviews

Hmmm feeling! It is strange! How do I answer the following question? My daughter, you have reached your third year, I had to start searching for the right school for you, and to be sure that you are in a suitable place all morning, and you are far from my eyes, and a new stage began with research and exams and waiting for the result.

Strange thing, how can a child of this age go through all this?

A new stage, a strange feeling, here we are starting to get serious...

I went with my mother, and I used her, especially since I was not driving the car even though I had a driver's license, but I was not driving...

The important thing is, we went to several public and private schools, and I always looked at the classrooms and the places my daughter would spend in the playground, the toilet, the smells emanating from it, cleaning and other things that surprised the school owner that I was not interested in the methods of study and others, but rather interested in these things.

My mom always told me I was weird with my decisions since I was young, I would see things the other way around and do them, well mom, thanks... lol.

My perspective on the subject is correct. It is necessary to achieve hygiene and psychological and physical comfort for the child. No matter how developed this curriculum is, it will not benefit if it does not provide the child with his comfort and rights; that is why I chose several schools, and made an appointment for the test.

I did not tell my daughter anything, but I prepared her for the situation. I told her: Listen, my love, today you will prove yourself, and make me happy if they choose you, and if they do not do that, do not be sad, because they will lose the most wonderful human being...

The night before the exam, I took her to the clothing store, and we chose the best formal clothes. Yes, a white shirt, a pink tie, a pink mini skirt, and black glowing shoes.

We went to the exam, I saw her radiate happiness when she saw the games, and she started having fun, and I was nervous, and I called her: Baby, come here, your clothes will be dirty.

The teacher asked me to leave her to measure how happy she is with the place, how she moves from one game to another, how she gets along with other children, and so on. Then we asked her to come and sit.

After extreme fatigue, we were able to prepare her for the exam, and the question appeared. I was much more nervous than her, but I controlled myself, and began to respond, and I was very surprised, I did not expect her quick response, and adaptation to the atmosphere of the school. The funny thing is that they wanted to know if she was fluent in French, so they asked her: What is said to the mouth in French? She said: (Booj) Ha-ha-ha, it is our slang, we say to the mouth (Puz) and my daughter said to them with all innocence (Booj) and so my daughter passed her first exam.

I cried that day, my feeling was indescribable, and my daughter finally started her life and became a kindergarten student (KG1).

I Thank you –oh Allah- for your blessings and for your endless giving towards every mother, father and child.

"I loved your self-confidence, self-love with your dear dignity, and I became content to tell you once what I want and you understand what I want.

What a wonderful girl you are".

School & Its Memories

You were 3 years old, girl, girl, I started studying at your school (KG1), I was happy with you, I see you wearing school clothes and shoes, and every day a different hairstyle ha-ha, you was tying your beautiful hair that fell on your back, coffee color with soft and flowing golden locks..

Your teacher was very happy with your hair, she loves it very much, and she loves to stroke your hair with her fingers. One day, and your teacher was talking to me, I told her that I wanted to cut your hair and make it short, but she did not like what I said at all. Do you believe? She prevented me from cutting it; you should be thankful to her, my love.

You also felt smart and cunning because of her love for your hair, so every time I did a nice hairstyle for you in the morning, you saw it completely open when you got home.

You were deliberately opening it, in order to increase your love for the school more and more. This is how you dress to attract the attention of the school to you, and you did, and the proof is that it prevented me from cutting your beautiful hair... Ha-ha, I adore you…

Another situation for you in (KG1), you were learning to leave the diaper, and you were smart, so you learned quickly, but you were not at school, and the funny thing is every day at a certain hour and at the same time you were hiding under the table, and you were doing your need, and the workers started cleaning and arranging, and so on in every one day it will be repeated, until you tell me what you are doing.

I remember how I sat with you, looked into your eyes, and calmly explained everything to you. I think you understood the topic, but you did what I told you. From that day onwards, I did not hear any complaints of this kind until I grew up and became the sweetest girl. I loved your self-confidence, self-love with your dear dignity, and I became content to tell you once what I want and you understand what I want. What a wonderful girl you are!

"I prefer to focus on the Arabic language, and at the same time encourage the child to acquire one or two languages in order to develop his skills and abilities in scientific fields; To adapt to the sciences of the future, and deal with them, does this mean the loss of his true identity?".

Lee Sulli

You started studying at KG1 and every day I teach you a word, and I hear you utter it, and I used to establish the world and make it sit out of my joy, and everyone knows that you uttered this word, how you pronounced it, in what style and all the minute details. My joy is indescribable, my little girl is able to utter words, and is able to formulate sentences. At your age, my dear, I had not yet entered school, and I was not aware of any word in Arabic or English, and now you are writing sentences in English, my joy in you.

In your school, you taught not only two, but three, including French. I can say: I was exploitative because I was the one who wanted to learn French and other languages, but I could not because I was busy with my work and studies at that time. I was hoping that you would study the language, and that you would help me learn and master it.

The problem is that not one of us masters the French language, and all of the homework is written in French, and I didn't know what to do, how to understand it, or study you?

I used the translation a lot, until I learned some words then.

The important thing is one day you and your grandmother were talking, and suddenly you said: (Lee Sulli), I looked at my mother, what does this girl say? My mother told me this is a French word, so I said: Maybe, oh my God! My daughter speaks French. and I used references, of course, and it dawned on me that it means (the sun), and when I showed her different forms of sun, moon and stars pointing to the sun, that was my happy day, and I was learning the first word in French (Lee Sulli)... Haha.

What did we learn from this story? Big and special dreams come true if you insist on implementing them, but do not expect everything you think to come true either.

I prefer to focus on the Arabic language, and at the same time encourage the child to acquire one or two languages in order to develop his skills and abilities in scientific fields; To adapt to the sciences of the future, and deal with them, does this mean the loss of his true identity?.

"And here you are singing the national anthem with all the divorce, enthusiasm and joy. I loved you at that moment, and I was happy with you, and I knew that I could count on you and that you would not let me down, my dear".

The Play of the Little Mouse

I do not remember the exact title of the play, but it is about a little mouse.

It's the school play, and every student in the class has a certain role to play, and that's the beauty of it. We all played the roles; in order not to generate any sensitivity in the classroom.

What is important is that my daughter played the role of a princess, and she had to wear elegant clothes with a crown on her head, and the supervisor of the play insisted, showing the clothes to each child in order to decide whether to change the clothes or not to change them.

I took for you the most beautiful red dress studded with crystals with a beautiful small crown that fits the clothes. When I showed it to the supervisor, she liked the dress very much, and said: Yes, that is what is required.

I was glad that they liked my taste, and I came home, and while I was sipping a cup of coffee, I got a call from the school. Do you know who she was?

She is the supervisor who called me to tell me that you have nominated you to present the national anthem on the stage, and asked me to train you to perform it correctly.

The days passed, and the day of the show came, and you wore the fluffy red dress studded with shiny crystals, with the hairdo (Carrie), and a small tiara inlaid.

I remember that I photographed you from home until you reached school, and everyone was looking at you as if you were an angel. How I loved this thing. Here I am lining up with all the families, and each of them sat in his place waiting for the performance, and I was afraid whether you would get better at singing the national anthem or not? The moment has come, the curtain has been raised, and here you are singing the national anthem with all the divorce, enthusiasm and joy.

I loved you at that moment, and I was happy with you, and I knew that I could count on you, and that you would not let me down, my dear.

You took your place in the play, and you finished your turn, and the curtain fell, and I came to you, remember? I was happy with you, and I took many pictures for the memory.

This is one of the important days that I will never forget. You were against me, and you did not want me to memorize anything, and you said: I know everything; That's why I didn't want to pressure you, and I left the topic to you, that's why I was afraid that you would do well on stage, and terrify people? But you were wow smart at the time, and you gained my trust.

In the end, the lesson of this story is to trust your daughter's abilities, and give her the opportunity to stand out and shine for herself without interference from you, oh mother, make her prove to you that

she is trustworthy.

"For bullying that gets too extreme, stop it from the start so you don't suppress feelings, and it turns into something bad".

The Golden Dress

You were four years old, and Eid al-Adha came, and you asked your aunt to sew golden clothes for you with a beautiful crown like her daughter, so that you would be beautified and appear like princesses on the day of Eid.

My darling, you liked the dress very much, and you wanted to wear it every time, and every time you were at home with your family, at parties and weddings, I didn't mind that I caused you pain for the same topic before.

Until the day of graduating from (KG2), from which she graduated at the age of four, and everyone classifies her at the age of five like them. That is why everyone with her in the class is older than her, and she is the only little one.

Unfortunately, the girls were laughing at her, or bullying her; because she is younger than they are, and this is what compelled me to go and speak to the administration to stop what is happening, and indeed everything has stopped, and all the girls have become the best friends and life companions until now.

The important thing is, I knew about the graduation party, and I prepared her purple clothe, but it was a normal dress. On the day of the party, you came - my love - and put on the golden dress that pissed me off and shouted at you that it is the salvation of clothing, and it is old, and this is a school that girls will not wear a dress for weddings.

I forced you to change clothes, and you were crying, I am sorry, but in moments I am harsh, I do what I want without feeling that I bother you, my love, so you changed your clothes reluctantly, and against your will, and we went by car, I don't remember if you remember, but you were sad for me, and you do not want to look me in the eye.

We got out of the car and walked, and we were walking. I saw the little girls wearing fluffy clothes, bags and shoes, and they were going to a wedding, not a graduation party, and then I looked at you my love, and sadness was visible on your face, because you would be the most beautiful, but I spoiled you...

I told you: they wear dresses, and you looked at me and said to you: I am sorry, my love.

But you are strong, my love, you went, played, had fun, shared and took the best pictures of you with your teachers and friends, and I thought that this would forget you, but unfortunately you did not forget.

That is what you are still saying: Did not I tell you everyone would wear a dress? You messed it up! Is not it? Mothers, instead of getting close to her, I prevented her from doing what she loves for the second time, and she still remembers, which means that he is in her heart and embarrassed her, and she will not forget. Wrong behavior. For bullying that gets too extreme, stop it from the start so you do not suppress feelings, and it turns into something bad.

"I believe that every child has a certain sense and a mysterious desire, and that he has the right to choose what he pleases, and we just have to bring him opportunities".

Men's Conquer

You were at the age of four or five, and your brother was at the age of two. We were using a BlackBerry phone in those days, and a message came to me stressing the need for children of your age to act in a short film called (Men's Conquer), and without any thought I submitted your names, and he came to me Reply quickly, yes your two children have been chosen to star in this movie.

I was happy; this was the first experience for you and me as well. I cared a lot about you and your brother. I was seeing everything that was new, and trying everything useful from a mathematical point of view, art, education, religion, everything.

If you sit and think with yourself, my love, you will see that you have tried everything, even the sport (gymnastics) that you love so much. And you have had enough of this sport and do not want to continue it. The important thing is, the promised day came, and I took you both from school, and they asked me to put you in shabby clothes, but my heart did not obey me.

The important thing is the place in Warqa area, in a villa that appears to be new, and no one has previously inhabited it...

Remember the story, my dear, all you had to do was play alone in the house, and the actor would come as your father, sit with you a little, and go to the room where his wife was waiting for him, so that the screaming and exchanging insults began; Because it did not provide her the previous luxurious life. She kept screaming at him, insulting him until he died of his oppression, and then your turn came again, they took him in the ambulance far away, and you stand with the world lost, lost looking at the ambulance that transports your father the actor...

I did not accept any dramatic quarrels in front of the children, nor did I accept offensive words in front of them, which made them, change the scenario so that they did not see anything of what was happening except playing and saying goodbye. Do not you see this, and it does not affect you either, even if it is acting.

Several weeks passed, and the time came for the film in which you appeared to be shown on the cinema screens as part of a competition for short films at the Dubai Film Festival in the halls of the (Festival City).

We took our positions, and all the parents are with us, and we waited when your turn came, how wonderful you were. My kids are on big screens hahahaha, yeah, and they have perfected their roles. The girl is playing, and the (hila hop) is cut for her, and the mucus I don't know where it came from, and you were improving it, you really looked shabby lol, this is the way of presenting and capturing the required moment and montage lol.

I believe that every child has a certain sense and a mysterious desire, and that he has the right to choose what he pleases, and we just have to bring him opportunities; to choose. What he loves cannot be abandoned or imagined, and when he answers the questions directed to him, he realizes that the things presented to him do not receive love in his heart.

I know after all these attempts you will be a great world skater.

"I cared about your mental health
more than anything else".

Listen the Words

You were stubborn, and I still am. I like this stubbornness. You took from your mother and father the trait of stubbornness and self-love. What I like is that you are fighting, nothing bothers you, and you do not let anything bother you, but when stubbornness is a cause for inconvenience, that is a different thing, my dear...

You have many situations with stubbornness, and not wanting to hear what I say…

I remembered well when I was young, maybe five years old, wanting to have everything, what is yours, and what is not yours, and you were crying so hard if you didn't get it, this thing bothered me so much that I wondered: What's wrong with it? I provide her with everything financially, morally and psychologically, so why does the girl not listen to my words? I had to be firm with you, you were crying so hard and hysterically. The thing that made me treat you unfairly, I was trying to catch you until I decided to leave you. And you fell on the ground, and you were hurt, but you didn't cry, but you looked at me in amazement, denouncing the thing that happened, you didn't expect me to leave you...

But I was not stingy with you, but I was against the acquisition of things that are harmful to you.

I cared about your psychological care more than anything else.

The important thing was just a moment until I decided that I would not cry again for trivial things. No one would be with me to support me if I insisted on stubbornness, but if I thought and analyzed the situation, and asked for what I wanted, I would get what I wanted, or I could be better than it.

This situation affected you a lot, my love, I can see its consequences in you now, you know what you want, you know how to get it, and most important of all that you do not let your right be confiscated from you until you get it.

This is how I want you to be strong, and I want you to advise your little sisters on this. For your life to be successful...

I remember your looks well, I knew that you would hate me for this, and you said it to me repeatedly, and I respected your frankness, and I told you that you are my daughter, and I must teach you self-reliance.

Petting, crying and wailing does not help, but self-confidence is what will benefit you in the future, and here are its consequences.

I am sure you will thank me for my toughness at that time with you...

I love you

"I learned the meaning of self-freedom and the desire to experience for the first time, and how to control my feelings as a mother, and how to accept these things, and deal with anger".

The Scouts

How wonderful to see your child come out of his shell, and on his own.

I remember you; you came to me and you were happy: Mom, look, I want two thousand dirhams for school, is that possible?! And why?! You showed me a paper that you want to participate in the school scouts. I was very happy, because I would have liked to be in the scouting ranks, but unfortunately the system was very complicated at the time. The important thing is to return to our topic.

I was very happy for her, she paid the required amount, and she joined the scouts.

On the second day, she came with a paper from school, and with the scouts' requirements. Let's remember together: sleeping bag, other travel essentials, toothbrush and more.

You were surprised, what is this? And why? The important thing is we went to the (Square Center) stores and bought all the supplies. Days passed, and you wore scouts' clothes on certain days, and I liked the pins visible in them.

The important thing is that one day you came with another message, and you told me about staying overnight. How do you sleep? My daughter who has never slept outside the house, and how do I agree to that? I started attaching all the required necessities to the accommodation, so I asked her: Do you really want to stay overnight? She said, "Yes, all my friends are going."

I said: Well, let's convince your father now, talk to him and convince him, and that's great. And I was counting the days, how would I let her go and sleep outside the house? The day came, and I packed her camping bag with all the equipment and supplies she needed. After school on Thursday, I took her to the second branch of the school in Al Barsha, and I also didn't want her to go. This is her first day out of the house, it should not be like this, it should be her wedding day, but I fulfilled her wish. She asked me to take her to the door, but I did not even notice that I could not, and drove her into the school. As usual, I got to know the official, I took the numbers and names, and the representative came, and asked me to leave.

It seems that I was embarrassing her, especially since I was the only mother in the school, I did not notice that, I did not notice that I was disturbing her atmosphere, and asked about their accommodation and food and so on.

I was embarrassing her, the important thing is that I left school, and left her with the scouts, but you didn't know that I stayed in the parking lot, I can't move, my eyes were fixed on the door looking at you long. I was trying to touch, look at you from afar, and get full of you. And when the time came, I left the camps, while I relied on God, and this is what you do not know is that I read Al-Ma'adat and Ayat Al-Kursi, and prayers for immunity and everything for you, and I look at the school, I pray for you safety, happiness and joy.

The important thing is that I did not sleep on that day. I felt that something was lost from me. I was praying and praying that you would be fine, and not feel cold. Who covers you when you get cold? Everything was in my head. I remember that day I slept late thinking of you.

You were happy, and this is what I wanted, I did not want to stand in your way at all, this is your time, and you can choose the life you want, but under supervision.

I slept sunken, tired, and the morning came, and I should have taken her at eight from the camp, and because I was tired, I fell asleep, and did not wake up. At nine o'clock the phone rang, I answered the call. I thought about her all night, I was late for her in the morning, I was supposed to be the first to take her and not the last, but I went and took her, and she was angry in a moment of silence. Come on tell me what happened, nothing happened, what did you do? We did nothing, still angry.

It is okay, I convinced her and things are good. The important thing is that I learned a lot here, I learned the meaning of self-freedom and the desire to experience for the first time, and how to control my feelings as a mother, and how to accept these things, and deal with anger.

"It is true that I am your mother, but I will not last you forever, as long as I live, I will not let any misfortune befall you, or any distress enter your heart".

What I Say for You?

One day I was in the living room, playing with my little girl, and if my older daughter looked at me, showing signs of discomfort, she asked me without any preliminaries: Is it true - Mother - that you did not breastfeed me as you did with my little brother and sister?

Astonishment appeared on my face, and my tongue was knotted with terror. How could she know this? It is my secret hidden deep inside, and I entrusted it to everyone from my family, my husband and everyone else, and I decided not to disclose the matter to anyone, so that she would not be able to hear it, but it seems that one of them spoke about it.

I wanted to comfort her, and explain my circumstances to her that it was because I was not in good health, and that she was my first child, my early experience. At the time, I was ignorant of the meaning of breastfeeding or patience for a child. I did not know anything at all; because the stress of pregnancy made me not aware of anything around me, as if I passed out from the many sedatives I was taking.

I explained to her my position, and I was watching her confused face, which did not understand what I was saying, as if she was saying: Be honest with me, Mom. It is the bitter truth, and since she knew this news from others, I must disclose the matter; I told her: I was going to tell you when you were a mother for the first time, then you would know what I felt, and I suffered, then you will know the meaning of all my feelings and I am unable to breastfeed you, but you are an integral part of me.

She was not convinced of this, and said: What is the reason, mother? She left me and went.

I had to find a way to convince her that she is the most precious thing I have, that she is my daughter and my life, and that she is the turning point in my life. I was unable to breastfeed her, but I was doing everything possible to give her a good life.

My dream was to be a successful businesswoman, and my determination to reach the highest levels; In order to give her everything she needs in the future.

After that, I became the mother of a son and two daughters. I became a breadwinner, ready to sacrifice everything for my children. I have had my successful and unsuccessful experiences.

At first I thought that I was a useless person, I ran after disappointment and behind the scenes of distress, and I thought that I could not accomplish what I had started; Because I simply lost hope, but no, then no, then no, that's how I repeated this word deep down. I must bring their future to the horizons of hope.

My daughter watches me from moment to moment while I am with her younger siblings, play with them, breastfeed the one, laugh with the other, and see her always absent-minded. I say to her: What is wrong with you, my daughter? She says: Did you sit with me like that, as you sit with them? Did you laugh with them like that you used to laugh with them? Did you breastfeed me, mother?

What do I tell her, my God? Guide me!

Finally, I said to her: Yes, I played with you with everything you loved, and laughed with you to this day, and if I did not breastfeed you, forgive me, my love, my daughter, because the circumstances were compelling for me.

She comes out again, I see her with tears in her eyes, and what a strong personality you have, my daughter, you did not wait for your tears to fall in front of me, do not make me feel that you are wounded and in pain. I got out before your tear drops! My love, my daughter...

I went to her, and sat next to her, and said to her: My child, my little girl, hear me well, It is true that I am your mother, but I will not last you forever, as long as I live, I will not let any misfortune befall you, or any distress enter your heart, I will leave life after I provide you with what you need after me, I promise you that, my love.

"When I carried you for nine months, I was tired of my pain, and I thought that I would not love you... And when I saw you, I forgot my pain, and I was glad because I am your mother, and you are my child".

My Tips for You

I have tips give them for you, so please listen them from me, and understand them; to climb the ladder of success, and be happy in your life whether I am alive or not.

Oh, apple of my eyes, my strength, my inspiration, every soul in my life, hear these my counsels of your early years; because it is the most important for your future and building your character.

Here you are, my child before my eyes, and time passes in the blink of an eye, you change, and you mature in all stages of your life.

One day you will be a mother and whether you are in your life or not, here are my tips:

When I carried you for nine months, I was tired of my pain, and I thought that I would not love you…

And when I saw you, I forgot my pain, and I was glad because I am your mother, and you are my child.

I advise you in your first year to laugh, and have fun, this is the time, and do not be sad.

In your second year, jump, play, it is time, and do not get tired.

In your third year, search, ask, this is the time, and do not be embarrassed.

In your fourth year, get ready, and learn, this is the time, and do not be absent.

In your fifth year, you know, be honest, it is time, and do not quarrel.

The years have passed, and I see you grow up, take care, build your character, and be proud of you, my love.

In your sixth year, seek knowledge, and be proud of your success, because this is its time, and do not be lazy.

In your seventh year, learn to respect your mother and father, this is his time, and do not frown.

In your eighth year speak politely and purity, this is his time, and do not scream.

In your ninth year, start mentioning your Lord, pray, and ask for Allah's mercy.

These are your early years, my dear. Learn, understand, concentrate, and finally just rest, my child.

Please do not let one subject be the reason why you do not enjoy life, you do not feel comfortable among those around you, do not be like that, my dear.

"I learned from this situation that she is a sensitive and shy girl, but she is strong and tough at the same time, and above all that she is very stubborn, and insists on her position as her mother".

Admonition scenes

Another scene of admonition, I could not control myself this time, because I raised her, and I hit her, what she did is unforgivable. And while I was with her, I threw a pillow on her, maybe it hurt her, maybe she got upset, or she was sad at the time. She rose and groaned at the top of her voice, asking me not to do this, and looking at me angrily. I could not help myself, especially that she did the same thing the day before, meaning that this was repeated over two consecutive days. She greeted me with screaming and anger, I said maybe she came from school, and she feels annoyed, and I put up with her intense screaming.

The situation continued for two consecutive days, to learn that she had no right to treat me in this way, even if I was wrong.

She withdrew from her hand (the mobile) and (the iPad) until she apologized to me, kissed my head, and told me that she was sorry, and she would not repeat this behavior again. I know my daughter well, she is strong, and she finds it difficult to apologize to anyone, and it was difficult for her to do what I asked her to do.

It came on the second day: Where is my mobile? I wanted to do homework and other things, but I refused. We stayed like this for two days, until one day she said to me: What is wrong with you, mother? Come on, give me the mobile, and I told her: I am still on my decision, you have to apologize to me.

I reluctantly kissed my head in embarrassment; and muttered with difficulty: I am sorry, Mom. It was clear that the reason for her apology was to collect what she had with me, and I was satisfied with her apology.

I learned from this situation that she is a sensitive and shy girl, but she is strong and tough at the same time, and above all that she is very stubborn, and insists on her position as her mother.

After we reconciled, and the situation deteriorated between us, I asked her about the reason for her distress and nervousness, and it turned out that this was due to her simple quarrels with her friends at school. The issue was not sensitive or important to interfere, and she left the choice to solve her minor problems with her friends.

"She's strong and nervous; it is not easy for her to tell me: Mom, I love you, but I could feel the strength of her love for me".

You Are My Eldest Daughter

I liked her attitude very much today, she has changed, she usually wears what she wants, gets angry, and does not hear the words, but she wears anything that is inconsistent, untidy and not ironed; To wake me up, and with all that her hair looks so beautiful, and she insists on not tidying it and leaving it frizzy; To annoy me, because when she was young I used to take care of her hair, learn new hairstyles for her, and when she grew up she hated everything I wanted to do for her. She thinks that in this way she is independent, and forms her own personality, far from my interest in her appearance.

The important thing is today I was going to meet a friend of mine, and I told everyone to get ready to go out, but I focused on her, took out her clothes, and she gave me a look, and I said to her: Look, I want you to appear in front of them in the most beautiful suit; Because you are my firstborn and distinguished daughter.

In order to get ready to go out, I let her get ready, and when I came back, I saw her, she put on her best clothes, arranged her hair and body, and put on her light makeup from the makeup box I bought for her, which was filled with beautiful, very light colors, highlighting her natural beauty with vegan colors suitable for her age. When I saw her, I knew that she loved me, and she did not know how to express this love, she is strong and nervous, it is not easy for her to tell me: Mom, I love you, but I could feel the strength of her love for me.

"Summary Dear mother, children go through strange moments and desires at this age; don't prevent them from trying the thing, and drawing conclusions from it if it suits them or not".

The Angry Hairstyles

You were ten years old at the time, and you moved from the children's section to the girls' section, and here my love has grown, and she was classified as a girl, how wonderful!!

You had and still have long, silky hair, like you (Rapunzel) from the Emirates. Every morning I see you with a new and very strange hairstyle. I was wondering where did you get these very strange hairstyles? And when I visited you at school, and saw the girls passing by me, each with a very frightening hairstyle, I realized then where my daughter invents different hairstyles; that's why she preferred to do her own hair without relying on me as she used to do in the past.

Worryingly, your hairstyles were fine, and I accepted them day after day, until your father noticed that, and began to prevent you from combing your hair in this way.

I felt that we were depriving you of this, although I did not mind. This is your decision, and one day you will realize the correct method and technique to master the art of hairstyles that you used to do; that is why I did not mind you refusing to help me. Your father forbade you, and you felt that you were sad, and you felt very angry, but you could not refuse his request.

I felt like he broke your mind, and from that day on you've just been brushing your hair like a ponytail. I tried a lot with you, it's okay, do what you want, I will talk to your father, but you are stubborn; Your sign is the Leo, and you will remain stubborn, as I think, forever.

Summary Dear mother, children go through strange moments and desires at this age;do not prevent them from trying the thing and drawing conclusions from it if it suits them or not. Do not get angry, and do not hold back, but watch and conclude to the end, and intervene if the matter calls for your intervention; to advice. Back to watch; in this way, you prove that you are strong, confident in yourself, and know right from wrong, and your steps in intervention will be quick and wise to correct the wrong.

"We – the mothers- must give our daughters a chance; for recuperation themselves up a bit, to reduce the fear of exams, and the tension they provoke".

Study for the Examination

You were ten, and the exams started. You had to stay at home; to study, and do not leave him. This is the examination system (no one goes out of the house).

They called me the executioner; for this reason. I had a business meeting at 6 o'clock in the Mall of the Emirates, and I had to go out. She told me -My mother- that you would come with me, and then I said: No, you have an exam, sit down and study. You said: I am tired of studying, and I will not study, but I want to go out.

I looked at her and said: I am going to work, and I will not go shopping or play at all. She said: it's okay, I just want to go out.

Well, she insisted, and I would be late for the meeting; I said to her: Well, but on one condition! She said: What is the condition?! Well, accept that you come with me, but that you bring your books with you. What?! Yes, yes, this is a policeman, I will take you to the restaurant after the meeting, eat and fill, and you will study for dinner. If you agree, hurry up, get ready, I will be late.

The important thing is that she reluctantly took with her the Arab book and the notebook, and got ready to go out.

The car was not a suitable place to give advice; because I wanted her out to be full of play and fun, and not to preoccupy her with heavy advice that would disturb her and her mood in those happy moments.

The important thing is that when we arrived, she attended the meeting with me, and sometimes I like to attend her as well; because I want her to learn trade from now on, in the event of my retirement she can take over the management of the company without problems. I finished the meeting, and we went to a restaurant of her choice; she loves steaks. We went to the African (Tribes) restaurant, it was my first visit, I loved the place, the name and the interior decoration, and I was asking about everything in the restaurant: What is this? How is that? And who is this? The thing that everyone gets upset about, my husband and kids, but I like to know a lot, and nurture my modest knowledge.

The important thing is that you annoyed me, and you did not like my many questions, so I remained silent, but on the other hand, the manager liked me, and asked the team to sing for us to receive us in the restaurant. This embarrassed her, and she said: I will not study then, so I looked at her, and said: Come on, open the book now, and let us see what you have. The important thing is that after we asked for food, we opened the book, and studied until the food came. The director was very impressed; and they sang to us again.

Here she said: I will not study. I smiled and said: Okay, let us start eating, and let's go home. We –the mothers- must give our daughters a chance; for recuperation themselves up a bit, to reduce the fear of exams, and the tension they provoke.

"When you see reality, fatigue and hard work in order to reach your goal, you will realize the meaning of the beautiful things in your life".

Work Appointment at IMG

Days pass, and things change in our lives. I remember that I transferred my project from electronic commerce to another job that I love, I feel the passion and want it, and I know that I will be creative in the world of events and organizing ideas. Yes, it has shifted from e-commerce to events. I was always keen when you were young that you would participate in my project, and I was keen to take you with me on every date I go to, but I wanted to start with you with a work date that would be hard for you, something you will love, I am sure of that.

The appointment came with the IMG Events Department, and I accompanied you, remember? In order to start the meeting, we had to start with an introductory tour, great, right?! We got special cards, and we started our tour. I remember you played all the games. The woman stopped me to explain to me about it, and I was happy lol. Is not it funny?

Because we are with the administration, we were able to go behind the scenes of the games, learn who is behind the mask, or how the game works and other things. I enjoyed this day, and I do not know what your feelings are? Tell me did you really have fun?

We completed the tour, and went to the offices. I remember that the employee was fascinated by my way of educating my daughter, as there are two professional steps that my daughter must follow, and to let her know about the difficulties that can be faced, and the method of dialogue and communication, and others. I looked at you, I saw you with amazement, games and fun, and in the back were ordinary and representative offices staring at her. I told her: When you see a reality, fatigue and hard work in order to reach your goal, you will realize the meaning of the beautiful things in your life.

This is the last paragraph for you mothers and daughters; to write your first memories with your daughters or with your mothers. Your books or your memories should be like a bell that rings from the past, reminding us of the future; because these memories will be forever.

____

____

____

____

____

____

____

____

____

____